The Orchestra

Written by
Paul Reeder

Illustrated by
Fraser Williamson

These are the violin players.

These are the trumpet players.

These are the drummers.

4

These are the flute players.

5

These are the tuba players.

6

This is the piano player.

This is the conductor.

8